MW01140308

CHUCKIE
SAYS
Goodbye

Copyright © 2021 Amy Jensen
All rights reserved.
ISBN: 978-0-578-31221-7

DEDICATION

This book is dedicated to Chuckie's sister, Neslee.

Thank you to everyone who helped make this book possible, especially all of Chuckie's fans! Thank you to my husband Roger, for being an amazing Dad to our fur children. Thank you to my friends and family for all of your love and support! Thank you to Cynthia for inspiring me to write this story.

And a very special thank you and lots of love goes to my collaborators Ulana Zahajkewycz and Amy Keller for helping to create such a special book with me.

Love, Amy Jensen

& Chuckie!

Hello, my name is Chuckie.

I am a chocolate lab.

My best friend was my sister,

The best I ever had!

Neslee was my sidekick;

We tussled all the time.

We went on walks, went swimming too,

We loved to jump and climb!

When someone was outside our house,

I'd bark to let her know.

And she would run right over,

To watch the people go.

Oh, she was calm and gentle,
With Bert she played so well.
I learned a lot from watching her,
What stories she could tell!

I remember how she teased me,
When I did something bad.
She liked to rub it in my face,
If I made Daddy mad.

One day I noticed Neslee,
Was struggling up the stairs.
Her legs were getting weaker.
She'd fall if we weren't there.

Sometimes Neslee made mistakes.

I know it made her sad.

But Mom and Dad would clean it up;

It didn't make them mad.

Mom and Dad and Bert and I,
All loved our girl so much.
We'd think of ways to cheer her up,
With hugs and treats and such.

She had some trouble eating,

So our parents helped her out.

She got so much attention,

That sometimes I would pout.

Daddy called a meeting.
We all sat by her bed.
Mom and Dad and Bert and I,
Gathered 'round and said,

How much she meant to all of us,
And all the things we felt.
Our love for her just filled the room,
We hugged her as we knelt.

Mom and Dad told all our friends,

To come and say goodbye.

She was so glad to see them,

Though sometimes they would cry.

People brought us cakes and snacks,

And some drew pictures too.

Love was all around our home;

It seemed each day it grew.

Grieving made us tired,
And we all took extra naps.
Some days we just forgot to eat,
Thank goodness for those snacks!

All too soon the day had come,

For us to say goodbye.

We spent the day with Neslee,

But the moments seemed to fly.

I feel so sad. I'm not myself.

I don't know how to be.

All I know right now is that,

My friend's not here with me.

Mom and Dad knew I was sad,
And took me to the park.
I went swimming in the creek.
I played 'til almost dark.

ACTUAL BUTTERFLY THAT
LANDED ON DADDY'S HEAD

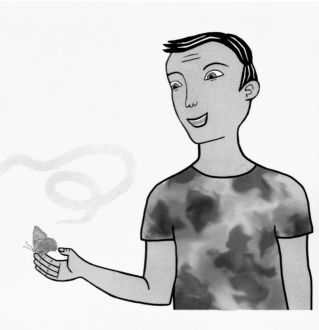

When I turned back from swimming,

A butterfly was there!

It landed right on Daddy's hand,

It landed on his hair!

Its presence made us happy,
'Twas such a nice surprise.
Like Neslee came to visit,
Then took off to the skies!

May our memories be a blessing,

Although we are apart.

We won't forget the ones we love,

We'll keep them in our heart.

Thank you, Neslee,
for being a very good girl!

NESLEE JENSEN
September 14, 2004 – June 19, 2018

Chuckie Jensen

Chuckie the Chocolate Lab is an extremely handsome and sometimes mischievous dog who loves his family, eating sushi, and going to the beach. He is a great brother and a kind hearted boy.

YOU CAN FOLLOW CHUCKIE!

Facebook:
Chuckie the Chocolate Lab
#TeamChuckie

Instagram:
chuckie_the_chocolate_lab_

Tiktok:
@chuckiethechocolatelab

About the Author:
Amy Jensen

Amy Jensen is the author of *Chuckie Makes Mistakes (Sometimes)*, *Chuckie Has A Bellyache*, and *Chuckie Says Goodbye*. She also teaches Vocal Music at Warren Middle School in Warren Township, NJ. This is her third children's book and collaboration with Ulana Zahajkewycz. Amy received the Excellence in Education Recognition Award in 2012. She earned her Bachelor of Music Education degree from Westminster Choir College and her Master of Curriculum and Instruction degree from the American College of Education. She lives in Bridgewater, NJ with her husband Roger and their fur babies Chuckie and Bernie.

Photo credit: KCW Photography

About the Illustrator:
Ulana Zahajkewycz

Ulana Zahajkewycz is a freelance illustrator and an adjunct professor at Moore College of Art and Design in Philadelphia, PA. She is also the co-owner of the Carnival of Collectables Antique and Art Mall, in Sicklerville, NJ. Ulana exhibits her art nationally and her print, "Murder She Wrote" is part of the permanent collection at the Frederick R. Weisman Museum of Art in Minneapolis, MN. Ulana lives in New Jersey with her partner Brian and their adorable cat, Underdog.

Graphic Designer: Amy Keller Please visit www.coroflot.com/Akeller to view her portfolio.

In Memory of our beloved Furry Friends

Apricot

Madden

Golden Benjamin

Cassis Preseau

Maddie Mac

Marty McFly

Mollie Mae

Bruno Berardi

Julius

Mr. Kittles

Doogie

Sabre

Bruno

LaLena

In Memory of our beloved furry friends

Molly Richardson MacGorman

Magnus

Wheatley

Stormi

Gus

Felix

Riley

BOOMER JONES

AMBER

WYNNIE MACGORMAN

TYBORN "TY TY" TYBERIUS

MAGGI

ARIEL & SEBASTIAN

MR. WINSTON

In Memory of our beloved furry friends

CYRUS

BROWNIE

LUCKY

LOLA

BUCA

CAMDEN

SOPHIE ADAMS

BUSTER

TESSE

EVE

MAYA DOODLE

MADI MAE

PRIEST

PUDDLES MADELEINE

photo credit: Madison Margaret Photography

HENNES

photo credit: Peerless Memories

In Memory of our beloved furry friends

CHARLIE

KOZKO

SIMBA

MOSES REPASKY

ZOEY

MADISON

KING

TIPS FOR DEALING WITH THE LOSS OF A LOVED ONE

 1 Draw pictures or write down your thoughts.

 2 Have a special ceremony to honor your pet or loved one.

 3 Share favorite memories of your loved one.

 4 Take nature walks or walks in your neighborhood.

 5 Collect money or donate items for a charity in their name.

 6 Understand that it is okay to cry, and that there will be happy and sad times.

 7 Remember to lean on your friends and family for support.

 8 Talking to a counselor can also be very beneficial.

 9 Be kind to yourself.

Add Your Own Photos Here
to the
Memory Pages: